THE LITTLE
VAN GOGH
IN THE BORINAGE

CATHERINE DE DUVE

HOW
VAN GOGH
BECAME
THE WORLD'S
MOST FAMOUS
ARTIST

 PÔLE MUSÉAL MONS   KATE'ART EDITIONS

At the time of Van Gogh

"The black country"

At the time of Vincent van Gogh, **the Borinage** was a prosperous region, thanks to the coal industry. This area in the West of **Belgium** was also known as the "black country", because of its mines, slag heaps, grey smoke and miners covered in coal dust.

The "Borains"– the local people – were originally peasant farmers. They were proud and loved their region, and spoke a dialect influenced by the Picard dialect of Northern France, known as "borain".

The workers, including women and children, mostly worked in the mines. But their living conditions were very tough. The work in the mines was very dangerous (accidents could happen) and unhealthy (no light, bad air-quality and epidemics such as typhus or cholera, etc.). The pay was terrible, and the working hours were long and exhausting. More than half of the workers couldn't read or write. The children didn't go to school as they had to help their parents.

What is this man wearing on his head?

Coal was used for heating, to power steam engines like steam trains, etc.

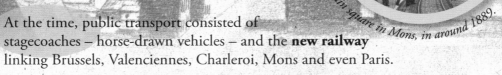

Mons is the capital of the province of Hainaut in Belgium. In 1878, its population was around 25,000.

The main square in Mons, in around 1889.

At the time, public transport consisted of stagecoaches – horse-drawn vehicles – and the **new railway** linking Brussels, Valenciennes, Charleroi, Mons and even Paris.

In the Borinage, Van Gogh found subjects which he would continue to paint throughout his lifetime: miners, weavers, peasants, cottages, etc.

 The houses with thatched roofs are cottages made of earth, wood and cob. What is the woman farmer doing?

Vincent

Vincent van Gogh was born on 30 March 1853 in Zundert in the Netherlands. His father, Theodorus van Gogh, was a pastor and had a great influence on him. His mother Anna Carbentus, a bookbinder's daughter, first taught him how to draw. Vincent was given the same name as his older brother, who had died. This was hard for him...

At the age of 11 he was sent to boarding school. It broke his heart to be separated from his family and he felt excluded. He left school at the age of 15.

His uncle Vincent, known as "Cent", gave him a job as an assistant in the **Goupil & Cie** art gallery in The Hague. There, Vincent discovered the world of art. For nearly six years, Van Gogh stored up in his memory the artwork which he handled there.

Imaginary Museum

Vincent was passionate about art. He visited museums and admired paintings by the great masters. He decorated his room with prints and created a small museum there.

As he spoke several languages, his family sent him abroad to work in the London and Paris branches of Goupil & Cie. Vincent, however, began to be more interested in religion than in his work. His withdrawn, surly character put off the customers, and he lost his job. What should he do now?

Discover Vincent van Gogh's imaginary museum.

Rembrandt

Millet

Delacroix

Hals

Rubens

Ruysdael

Evangelist

1. England

Through an advertisement, Vincent found a job as a schoolteacher in England. He also taught Sunday school classes and sometimes preached in the churches in **Richmond**. When visiting **London**, he was struck and deeply shocked by the abject poverty in the workers' districts. At the age of 23, Vincent discovered a new vocation: he wanted to become a pastor, like his father, or a missionary. His family, somewhat puzzled, sent him to work in a bookshop in **Dordrecht**. He'd get over it...but Vincent did not get over it, and his father finally came round to the idea.

2. Amsterdam

Van Gogh moved to Amsterdam. He began to take classes in Latin, Greek and religious texts such as the Bible, as a preparation for studying theology. He found his studies very boring; now and then he could slip out to go and admire the paintings by **Rembrandt*** in the museum. Maybe these studies were too difficult? Later on he wrote that this was the worst time of his life. Vincent gave up his studies.

This is the "Au Charbonnage" café, where local workers came for some bread and a glass of beer.

🔍 Look at this sketch, which Vincent made when he was not yet very skilled. He used a thick pencil, pen and ink. The perspective is not quite right.

3. Brussels

His father went with him to Brussels to enrol him in a missionary school in **Laeken**. Vincent studied there for a trial period of three months, but he was not disciplined enough and was not allowed to continue his training as a missionary. What should he do? During his time in Brussels, Vincent visited the Royal Museum of Fine Arts, with his brother Theo. Later, along the Charleroi canal, he came across the "Au charbonnage" café. He "scratched out a picture" of it, as he put it, on a piece of paper, folded the paper in half and sent it, together with a letter, to Theo. He wanted to make quick sketches of things he saw when he was out and about.

The Borinage

Houses Borinage designed by Van Gogh.

People like Van Gogh were being asked to come to the Borinage to evangelize the local people. Vincent looked up the region in a geography book and set off straight away to try his luck there! He arrived in December 1878, and in February 1879, although he had no qualifications, was taken on for a six month trial period as a house-to-house evangelist and religious education teacher in a small Protestant community. He could throw himself fully into his new vocation. Vincent was very fervent. His family and friends were worried. He wanted to live like Jesus among the poor. And there was a lot of work to be done, healing the sick and wounded and comforting widows and orphans. For two years Vincent lived among the miners.

For years now, Vincent had been drawing sometimes for pleasure. He sketched his landlord and landlady as they went about their work, and made pencil drawings of the landscapes around the mine. He gave away his drawings, which often ended up being used to light fires in the cottages...

"… it was in the Borinage that I began to work from nature for the first time", he wrote later to his friend, the painter Eugène Boch, who came from La Louvière, not far from the Borinage.

This is a watercolor painted by Van Gogh in 1879. Can you see the factory, its chimneys and the slag heaps?

Abroad

When Vincent arrived in the Borinage, he stayed a few days with the Vanderhaeghen family in a hamlet called Pâturages. He then rented a room, which he shared with the children of the farmer Jean-Baptiste Denis in Wasmes, closer to the mines. Vincent felt that this was too comfortable, so he moved to a squalid hut in Wasmes. He wanted to give up everything, and distributed his money, his clothes and his shoes to the poor. He stopped washing and slept in his daytime-clothes. Vincent looked more like a beggar than a preacher!

Van Gogh preached in a small hall – the *Salon du Bébé* or *Temple du Bébé* – in the rue du Bois in Petit-Wasmes. But he was not very good at speaking in public, nor at organising religious meetings to bring comfort to the local people. He was not a popular preacher. Also, this Dutchman didn't understand the local dialect, which was spoken too quickly for him, and the "Borains" didn't understand his high-brow French.

They used to chat about Van Gogh. Do you understand what they're saying, in their local dialect?

– "Bah, i n'a rié avec ça! El rou flamind a dit l'aute jour : les geins paüfes sont pus hûreux."
– "Ouais, el rou, il a dit : "hûreux dins leu tiète mais nié dins leu pormonnaie!"

Translation : – "But that's nothing! That Dutch red-head vicar said the other day that poor people are more blessed". – "Yeah", the red-head said, "their minds might be blessed but not their wallets…".

The black country

It's winter, and the "black country" is covered in snow. This is a procession of "scloneuses", the women whose job it is to transport the coal out of the mine. Their ragged clothes are as black as the coal. Can you hear them? What are they talking about as they struggle on, weighed down by the sacks of coal? What do they think of Van Gogh the preacher?

In July 1879, Vincent's contract as an evangelist (lay minister) was not renewed. Depressed, he went to visit his parents at Etten. His family suggested that he should become an apprentice, to learn the job of a carpenter, an accountant or a baker... His father despaired and even thought of sending him to a mental asylum. When he came back to Cuesmes, he admitted that he had failed. He didn't know what he wanted to do with his life. He was in despair! So he packed up his drawings of miners and walked all the way to Brussels. He went to visit Pastor Pietersen. Back in the Borinage, Vincent rented a nicer, lighter room.

This house is called La maison Magros. Vincent drew it in charcoal. Can you see that it's leaning over a bit? Imagine the life of the person who lives in this house.

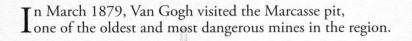

In March 1879, Van Gogh visited the Marcasse pit, one of the oldest and most dangerous mines in the region.

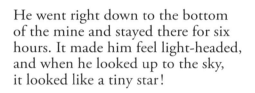

He went right down to the bottom of the mine and stayed there for six hours. It made him feel light-headed, and when he looked up to the sky, it looked like a tiny star!

What did he see in the mine? Five floors of galleries, and a stable with seven horses, 700 meters underground.

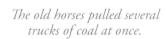

The old horses pulled several trucks of coal at once.

He also saw the exhausting work of the miners, breaking off the coal with a pickaxe, lit only by a small lamp, sometimes flat on their stomachs on the ground.

← *There were often accidents in the mines: gas explosions, such as the infamous firedamp explosions, rockfalls, flooding, collapsing galleries...One month after Van Gogh's visit to the Marcasse pit, there was an explosion in the Agrappe mine near Frameries, and 121 people were killed.*

An explosion in the Agrappe mine.

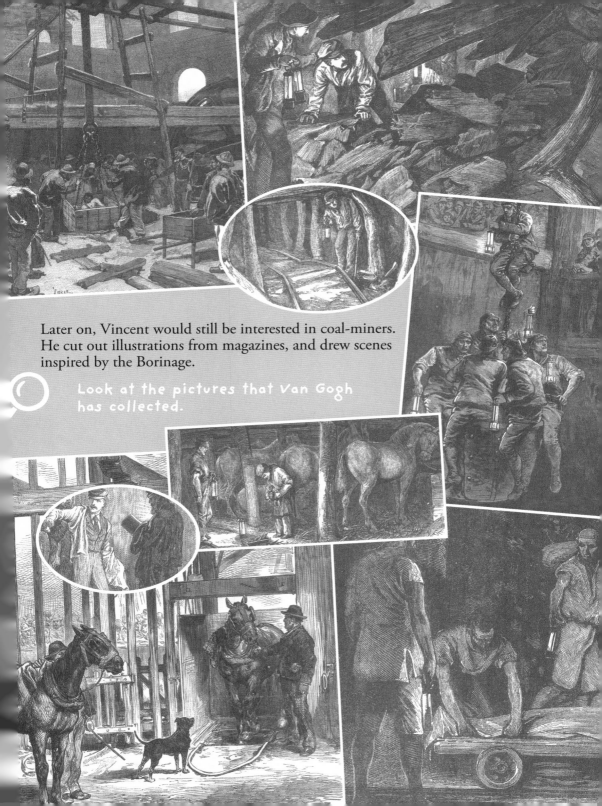

Later on, Vincent would still be interested in coal-miners. He cut out illustrations from magazines, and drew scenes inspired by the Borinage.

Look at the pictures that Van Gogh has collected.

Courrières

In early March 1880, Van Gogh packed his bags and left the marshes of Cuesmes to go to Courrières, in the department of Pas-de-Calais in France. Van Gogh was following his intuition! He wanted to meet up with the painter Jules Breton who he had met at the Goupil gallery in Paris. He loved Breton's paintings.

Jules Breton (1827-1906)

Van Gogh took the train to Valenciennes and then continued on foot. He loved walking, and put up with the freezing rain and wind. In spite of the storm, Vincent carried on bravely. Nothing would stop him! For three days and three nights he passed through towns and villages and camped in the middle of fields. At night he took shelter in abandoned carts, beside piles of logs or in the dip of a haystack.

Imagine and draw the countryside which Van Gogh travelled through on his way to Courrières.

Market square of Courrières

Jules Breton's house

The brewery

The church

When he reached Courrières, the town didn't look as he thought it would, but, instead, more like a mining town. There was nobody in front of Breton's studio. Vincent thought the building looked unwelcoming and didn't dare go in. He left for home with nothing to show for his journey, and still had to walk another 70 kilometers.

What has Van Gogh put in his suitcase? It's probably full of drawings just like the ones he swapped during the journey for some food.

Look at these two sketches. In the snow, miners are making their way to the pit. What are they carrying? Can you see the coalmines?

Weavers

On his way to Courrières, Vincent van Gogh passed through villages mostly inhabited by weavers. He was amazed by their skills, and found them "indescribably beautiful".

Vincent admired this shadowy trade; the men and women winding the thread onto the rollers, activating the shuttles, crossing the weft yarn and the warp yarn. Their movements were very precise. Later, in the Netherlands, he met more weavers, who he drew and painted. The artist shows how beautiful they really are.

At the time, the trade of weaving flax at home was starting to die out. Gradually, the weavers were being replaced by the mechanical looms of the new textile industry. The weavers worked in their cottages or in cellars of beaten earth, which were poorly lit, narrow and cold, to keep up humidity levels, and so make the thread stronger. The pay was very poor – not enough to live on.

 Can you find the roller, the shuttles, the oak loom, and the pedals in these pictures?

An ABC of drawing

In Cuesmes, nature was about to burst into flower and Vincent's energy was returning too. In fact, Van Gogh wasn't naturally talented, but he was keen to improve. He asked his brother Theo to send him reproductions of works by **Jean-François Millet** so he could copy them. Artists starting out often learnt to draw by copying other people's work.

With the help of drawing manuals, Vincent also practised drawing nudes with charcoal. This taught him about the proportions and positions of the human body.
Van Gogh worked very hard, tirelessly repeating the exercises again and again.

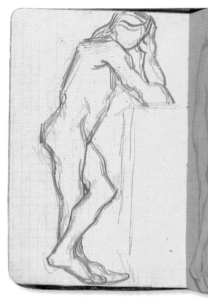

Look at Van Gogh's drawing of Bargue's model. Now it's your turn! Have a go, and write your name under your sketch.

Bargue

Van Gogh

Anatomy and Perspective

In August 1880, after some hesitation, Van Gogh decided to become a painter! He had found a meaning for his life. Theo also believed in him and had begun to send him money by post. Van Gogh could work on his art, buy paper, crayons and ink and live on a modest income. He sent letters to his brother telling him about his work.

Charcoal

He also studied a **book on perspective**. Once he had read this book, Vincent managed to draw a kitchen scene, of which he was proud.

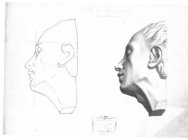

Charles Bargue

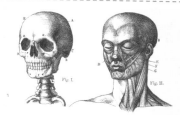

Albert von Zahn

It's your turn! Draw your own kitchen, taking care with the perspective.

Armand Cassagne, An ABC of Drawing

Brussels

A s he had often done before, Van Gogh suddenly moved elsewhere. In October 1880, he left the Borinage for good and settled in Brussels.

Vincent wanted not just to live surrounded by museums and art galleries, but also to meet other artists. And, at the end of the nineteenth century, Brussels was a good place for art.

Charleroi canal

Van Gogh rented a room opposite the South Station and enrolled in the **Fine Arts Academy** in Brussels. He was the oldest student; he took an exam but got the lowest mark...So he preferred to share a studio with his young Dutch friend Anthon van Rappard, and to take private lessons in perspective.

This is Brussels at the time of Van Gogh. Spot the Palais de Justice, built by the architect Joseph Poelaert between 1866 and 1883.

Pen and ink

Vincent was making progress. His figures had more volume and were more expressive. He got the proportions right. The artist was developing his own personal style. He used ink and various thicknesses of nib to create the effect of different textures.

Look at the drawing. Where are we?
Find where the details fit in and describe
what is going on. Also, look at the different pen-strokes.

Learning from Millet

Of the artists which Van Gogh admired the most, **Jean-François Millet** (1814-1875), one of the leading artists of the "Barbizon School", was one of his favorites. Vincent learnt a lot by copying reproductions of Millet's paintings. Like him, Van Gogh wanted to portray the life of peasants on the land.

In 1880, Theo sent his brother ten pictures from the series "Travaux des champs" (Work in the Fields) by Millet. Vincent made exact copies of them. Years later, he would make free copies of black and white engravings, increasing their size and using very bright colors.

Compare Millet's engravings with Van Gogh's paintings. Which technique do you prefer?

Barbizon School: Barbizon was a hamlet near Fontainebleau, in France. Between 1825 and 1875, a group of painters (Millet, Corot, Daubigny and Rousseau) wanted to draw what they could see, so they worked directly, outdoors.

What are these people doing?
What work are they doing?

21

The Sower

Vincent van Gogh especially liked Millet's Sower, in which the artist studied the sower's gestures very carefully.

Copy the man's gesture. Can you feel how he is connecting the sky and the land?

Now it's your turn! Draw a man sowing seed in the style of Millet, then add colors, as Van Gogh did!

1873 ↑

1890 →

23

Potato eaters

In 1881, Vincent moved to **The Hague**. There he took painting lessons from the famous Hague School artist Mauve, his cousin by marriage, who encouraged him. Thanks again to Theo, Van Gogh set up a studio, where he lived with his companion Sien – a mother with two children. She modelled for him and he wanted to marry her. He thought that marriage would help him to lead a more balanced and happier life. But his family were very shocked by the idea! So Van Gogh had to break off the relationship.

Vincent went to **Drenthe**, then back to his parents' house in **Nuenen**, where he stayed for almost two years, renting a studio. In Nuenen, the young artist was surrounded by Dutch village life. What did he see there? Vincent was interested in the lives of the peasants. What was their life like? What did they talk about? What did they eat? He observed their family-life very closely. Crouching in the corner of the cottage, Vincent made many studies of heads and hands.

Bon appetit!

In 1885, Vincent produced his first large-scale painting with several figures! It shows an evening scene, by the low light of an oil lamp. The light and shadows make the faces even more expressive. Vincent compared the color of their faces to a "really dusty potato, unpeeled of course".

Tick tock... What time is it in the De Groot family house? Go into the cottage. Listen to the conversation. Yum yum.....something smells nice! The food is hot and steaming. What are those women in white caps doing? What are they eating and drinking? Would you like to share their meal?

Look at this large picture. Imagine the conversation they are having around the table.

Academy and Studio

Antwerp

After his father died, Vincent went to live in **Antwerp** in Belgium. There he visited the cathedral and discovered the great paintings by Rubens*. He enrolled in classes in the **Fine Arts academy**, but wasn't happy with them. His teachers, moreover, didn't think he was suited to the classes. He was the laughing-stock of the studio. After three months, Vincent left Antwerp to go somewhere new... Paris!

Antwerp

* To find out more, read The Little Rubens, *in the same collection*

Paris

Van Gogh went to join Theo in Paris. He stayed there for two years. In the museums and churches he again came across the great painters he so much admired. Vincent collected **Japanese prints***, which inspired him. He copied them, heightening the contrast between the colors. He started spending time at the Fernand Cormon studio. There he met other young artists such as Toulouse-Lautrec, **Bernard, Pissarro and Guillaumin**, with whom he became friends. Vincent discovered the techniques used by the Impressionists and the Pointillists. He gradually began to move towards this new way of painting. He used lighter colors and thicker brush-strokes. He painted flowers, **Montmartre** and his first self-portraits. He worked side by side with the Pointillist painter Signac and exhibited his work here and there. Vincent met Gauguin, who fascinated him, just like his father used to do.

* To find out more, take a look at The Little Van Gogh *and* The Impressionists' Japan from Monet to Van Gogh.

A "painting-locomotive!"

Arles

In February 1888, Van Gogh left Paris. He headed for the sun, the light, the bright colors. He stopped in Arles in the South of France and, after two months, rented the **"Yellow House"** on the Place Lamartine. He wanted to create a house for artists (*L'Atelier du Midi*). Only Paul Gauguin* joined him, at Van Gogh's insistence. In the meantime, Vincent worked in the open air, "like a painting-locomotive"! He quickly produced a whole series of paintings of fruit trees in blossom and sunflowers, to decorate the house, even his bedroom. He used contrasting colours such as blue and orange. After an "electric" discussion with Gauguin, Van Gogh suffered his first mental breakdown and cut off a part of his own ear.

Look at all the objects which Vincent has put in his room to make him feel at home. Which colors has the artist chosen for his bedroom?

*To find out more, take a look at The Little Gauguin, in the same collection

Exhibitions

Anna Boch

Eugène Boch

Vincent van Gogh was invited to show his paintings at the *Salon des XX** in Brussels. An article was published praising his work. Anna Boch, a painter and the sister of his friend Eugène, bought a picture, "The Red Vineyard", from him for 400 francs. Van Gogh also exhibited at the *Salon des indépendants* in Paris.

Salon des XX: In 1883, a group of twenty artists created the "Group of Twenty". These included artists such as Khnopff and Ensor, who, a year later, organized the first "Salon of the Twenty" and issued invitations to artists such as Monet, Van Gogh, Gauguin, Rodin and Seurat.

Salon des indépendants : Set up in 1884 in Paris to enable artists to exhibit freely, without the restrictions imposed by the traditional jury of the Salon de Paris. Its founder members included Seurat and Signac.

Saint-Rémy-de-Provence

In Saint-Rémy, he painted several colored copies of black and white prints by painters he admired (Delacroix, Rembrandt and Millet). He gave them the colors he could see in his imagination.

In May 1889, at his own request, Van Gogh entered the **Saint-Paul-de-Mausole** asylum at Saint-Rémy-de-Provence near Arles. He could no longer cope with his crises, when he became very disturbed, even swallowing tubes of paint and turpentine.

*To find out more, take a look at The Secret of Fernand Khnoppf, *in the same collection.*

Auvers-sur-Oise

A year later, Vincent left the asylum and spent a few days in Paris, before settling nearby in Auvers-sur-Oise. There, **Doctor Gachet** promised to look after him.

Vincent worked for ten weeks but felt very lonely. He went back to see **Theo**, who had married Johanna. Vincent had become godfather to their son Vincent. But that summer, Vincent got hold of a pistol and shot himself in the chest. Two days later, he died in the arms of his brother Theo, on 29 July 1890. Theo died six months later. They were eventually buried side by side.

Look at this portrait of Dr. Gachet. What's he thinking about? Which flowers can you see?

Cottages

Throughout his life, Vincent van Gogh liked to paint ordinary houses. He was struck by how picturesque they were, these cottages and huts where the miners, weavers and farmers lived, scattered here and there – along the little paths in the woods or on the hillsides. In the evenings, warm light filtered through the small panes of glass at the windows. They looked so welcoming!

Look at these houses. Which one do you like best?

The Borinage
1879-1880

Scheveningen
1882

Loosduinen
1883

Nuenen
1885

Les Saintes-Maries-de-la-Mer
1888

Auvers-sur-Oise
1890

Anyway, for me the most wonderful thing
that I know in terms of architecture is the cottage with
a mossy thatched roof, with its blackened hearth.
Vincent van Gogh, *Letter 809*

Wherever Vincent went, he painted little houses.
Was he looking for a home, where he could finally
paint in peace?

Text: Catherine de Duve
Concept & coordination: Kate'Art Editions & the Foundation Mons 2015
Factual editing: Sjraar van Heugten, Caroline Dumoulin, Aukje Vergeest, Arnaud Godart, Alice Cantignau
Design: Véronique Lux
Editing: Marie-Christine Norbert
Translation: Rachel Beasley

With thanks to: Sjraar van Heugten, curator of the exhibition *Van Gogh in the Borinage* (BAM 2015), Aukje Vergeest, Pierre Tilly, researcher and lecturer at UCL, Pierre-Olivier Laloux, historian, lecturer in English at the Université Saint-Louis and at the EPFC, Xavier Roland, director of the Pôle muséal, Caroline Dumoulin, project manager at BAM, Véronique Lux, Anne Desclée, Claude Gérin, Bregje Provo and all those involved in the production of this book.

A joint production of Kate'Art Editions, the Mons 2015 Foundation and City of Mons